Empowered Marketing

Empowered Marketing:

Creative Strategies for Church and Non-Profit Marketing

Anthony Scott

www.empoweredmarketing.org

Table of Contents

DEDICATION

This book is dedicated to the memory of my mother, Zelphia P. Scott, who I lost to cancer at a very young age. During our time together here on this earth, she poured a wealth of wisdom and life lessons into me that still carry me until this very day. I will always love and miss her.

I also dedicate this book to my father, Robert Scott, who personifies diligence, perseverance and never giving up despite the circumstances. He has made many sacrifices on my behalf and this book is just one way of expressing that his investment in me is paying off.

Lastly, to my son Joshua who gives my life meaning and purpose. May this book be a testimony and example to you that you can achieve ANYTHING you set your mind too. This is just one contribution to the incredible future I envision for you.

ACKNOWLEDGMENTS

It's been said that a leader is only as good as his team or as wise as his mentor. I'd like to acknowledge a few special people who inspire me towards success. First, I'd like to acknowledge my pastor, Bishop T.D. Jakes who has been a source of mentorship and inspiration to me over the 7 years I've served God through his ministry. It's the Bishop's "Live on Purpose" attitude and spirit that motivates me to pursue my passions and dreams. This book is one of them.

I also want to acknowledge my fellow church and non-profit workers and volunteers who dedicate countless hours to important missions and visions that make a difference. I applaud you and celebrate you on your choice to move from success to significance.

Lastly, I couldn't do anything without the support of my family and friends. My dear friend and strategic advisor, Kim Drayton, thanks for being a tremendous blessing. Also, to all of my encouragers, coaches and prayer warriors including Juanita MacBeth, Jason Caston, Darcie Davis, Limmie Tyler, Nate McLaughlin and Deborah Phillips, thank you for the support! To the countless other friends and supporters as well as those I have trained… you mean the world to me. I appreciate the confidence you have in me as I pursue this and other ventures.

Introduction

In an economic environment where ministries and nonprofit organizations are struggling to identify and implement new and innovative strategies to sustain growth and position themselves as relevant, I felt compelled to write this book in an effort to help them further their causes and expand their outreach.

As a marketing professional with over 20-years experience in both corporate and nonprofit marketing, I have had the opportunity to leverage my experiences to create an effective model for delivering effective, strategic marketing campaigns for The Potter's House of Dallas, Texas and T.D. Jakes Ministries.

I had an opportunity to share some of these strategies with pastors and leaders from across the globe at several standing room only marketing sessions at The International Pastor's and Leadership Conference

2011 and 2012.

During these sessions, I discussed the unique challenges and nuances that both ministries and non-profits face in the marketing realm and provided some key strategies to help leaders, responsible for this aspect of their organizations, leverage their current efforts.

During the Q&A sessions, I realized that the needs of the audience ranged from understanding basic marketing concepts to more complex strategies like how to measure the effectiveness of a campaign. This book is in response to the many questions I received during my sessions and the questions I receive from ministry and non-profit marketing professionals on an ongoing basis.

The premise of this book is that marketing can be a key factor and effective tool for both ministries and non-profits regardless of the organization's size. But, surprisingly, I often encounter some resistance to "churches doing marketing" or am confronted with assertions that "non- profits are losing their focus" or "going commercial". So let's talk about this briefly.

Some schools of thought argue that churches should not market "the gospel" while others argue that marketing is a sure-fire way to "spread the gospel". When it comes to church marketing, I always refer to a critical source for direction and inspiration...The Bible. Consider the following scripture that I feel gives some unique insight on the subject.

Luke 16:8 (MSG) – *Streetwise people are smarter in this regard than law-abiding citizens. They are on constant alert, looking for angles, surviving by their wits. I want you to be smart in the same way—but for what is right—using every adversity to stimulate you to creative survival, to concentrate your attention on the bare essentials, so you'll live, really live, and not complacently just get by on good behavior."*

For me, this means we should use any and every tool at our disposal to help us effectively get the word out, be it for ministry or promoting a good cause. This scripture is saying that the secular or business world really gets this principle and this is the one instance where we could really learn from the way things are done in "the world".

I often consider Jesus and His disciples as the first and most consummate "marketers". Jesus attracted crowds of more than 5,000 people and implemented a unique strategy to spread the Gospel that's still effective more than 2,000 year later.

What marketing principles did Jesus demonstrate?

1. He recruited disciples (Sales)
2. People were talking a b o u t h i m (Word-of-Mouth Advertising)
3. Person-to-person interaction via the disciples (Direct Marketing)
4. Miracles and radical teaching (demonstrations & promotions)

5. Sampling (Psalm 34:8 NKJV – Oh, taste and see that the Lord is good; Blessed is the man who trusts in Him!

Regardless of where you stand on ministry or non-profit marketing, my real goal in writing this book is to provide information...basic strategies for churches and non-profits to use, even if you're operating on a shoestring budget.

This book is ideal for marketing directors, non-profit board members, committee chairs or volunteers who have been tasked with providing marketing direction or support for a church or non-profit organization. It's time to use any resources readily available to assist you in furthering your mission of making a difference and changing lives for the better. Be blessed, encouraged and equipped as you go forth.

The next chapter of the journey begins now...

Chapter One:

What Is Marketing?

"Everything you say, everything you do, from the moment you conceive of your idea to the point in time which consumers become repeat customers is marketing." - Jay Conrad Levinson

Before we begin our discussion about "Empowered Marketing", let's jump straight to the basics and define what marketing is. I know this chapter may seem a little too basic for some, but please indulge me for a quick refresher.

I've come to discover that many churches and non-profit organizations, particularly those with limited resources, don't have full-time marketing or development staff. As a result, some of these entities rely on the kindness and expertise of volunteers or board members, who in some cases, may or may not have a marketing skill set.

So, to be on the safe side, let's define marketing. Although there are hundreds of detailed books written on the subject of marketing by various scholars, experts and business leaders, I wanted to simply turn to the dictionary for the most basic and relevant definition I could find. According to Webster's, Marketing is: *The provision of goods and/or services to meet customer needs.*

Another definition that I absolutely love is from Jay Conrad Levinson of "Guerrilla Marketing" fame. He states:

"Everything you say, everything you do, from the moment you conceive of your idea to the

point in time which consumers become repeat customers is marketing."

This is where we officially begin our discussion about marketing for churches and non-profit organizations. Your marketing could include bulletins or newsletters. Perhaps it's a public service announcement on a local television station or running radio spots to promote a special service. It could be the sign on your vans or buses or even the sign outside your facility. Maybe you're running ads in the newspaper or you have a website that you're trying to get people to visit.

These are all common marketing elements and tools employed by churches and non-profit organizations. Marketing is many of the things you're doing already to help get the word out about your organization. The information you will find in this book is meant to empower you and spur your creativity towards these continuing efforts for greater success.

Now that we have a basic definition of what marketing is, let's talk about what marketing is NOT. For example let's consider something basic, like an informational flyer. Some say this is marketing. In truth, this IS a form or tool of marketing, that's communicating some information to a potential customer/client. The real POWER of truly understanding what marketing is, however, is to go deeper and take this a step further:

- Who is the flyer going to?
- How many people will see it?
- What specifically will your flyer say or promote?

Next, let's determine…

- What do you want the reader to do?
- What is the desired outcome from the flyer?
- What does success look like for this effort?

This is marketing. A tool or process that helps you take a solid, strategic look at what you're planning to do; establish what you hope to achieve; and position you to do it in such a way that maximizes your resources and results. Anyone can design a flyer, but what is your goal in creating it? Is it to inform, encourage an action or provoke a response?

The marketing process begins with the right questions that ultimately lead you to your strategy. This is what I call "Empowered Marketing".

This is the goal of Empowered Marketing:

- To challenge you to look deeper at what you're already doing and to do it in such a way that gets you a desired result.

- To challenge you to have a purpose or strategy in mind with all of your marketing efforts, whether they are large or small.

- To have a realistic expectation of what success looks like before you launch

- To recognize that everything you release into the public domain is a direct reflection of you!

- To utilize every modern resource available to help you achieve your goals

THE MARKETING PROCESS:

There are three basic parts to the marketing process:

1. **Research:** taking a deep look at your industry.

2. **Analysis:** analyzing, reviewing and processing the research you secured.

3. **Strategies & Tactics:** making decisions, based on your analysis, on how to proceed and the best ways to implement your strategies.

Research

"Wisdom is the principal thing; therefore get wisdom: and with all thy getting get understanding." – Proverbs 4:7

Research helps you learn more information about your "customer", your competition, your industry, the latest trends in your field and your overall market potential.   This information is a vital part of any marketing effort. Research challenges you to ask questions about "you". In other words, what sets you apart from the competition or what opportunity is not being addressed by the competition?

Solid research offers a profound opportunity to recognize your own unique Features & Benefits as an organization:

What is a feature?

A characteristic of your business, ministry, product or service

Example: items that make your ministry unique such as service times, ministry options available and location

What is a benefit?

What does the "feature" DO FOR or GIVES TO the customer?

Example: things that motivate people to visit you such as convenience of your location, opportunities to serve, giving comfort, enhancing spiritual well-being, inspiration

Time and experience has proven time and time again that people are moved by benefits, not features. Understanding the unique benefits YOU offer ultimately helps determine your positioning.

Positioning

Marketing is ultimately about "positioning" – the way you establish your product, service, organization or brand in your customer's mind so that they think of YOUR organization or brand ahead of others. For example:

- What's the first company that comes to mind if I tell you I need new tires? What's the first brand you think of?

- What's the first thing that comes to mind if I asked you about a charbroiled fast-food hamburger?

- Fill in the blanks: Like a good neighbor _____ _____ is there!

What do people think of when they hear your organization's name?   You can have a significant impact on the answer through positioning.

Analysis

Analysis or evaluation of your research is important to help uncover valuable information or trends related to the organization or its services to make judgments that ultimately help determine your strategy. Without getting too in-depth in this area, there are two primary types of analysis: Quantitative and Qualitative analysis.

For quantitative analysis, the most common approach for this basic level of analysis is dissecting your research results into charts, graphs, tables or averages for a visual representation of your research and discoveries from a mathematical perspective. For example: *We saw 235 new donations this year over last year, representing a 25% increase in donations compared to the previous year.*

For qualitative analysis, the focus is more on the details or how and why of consumer behaviors and the researcher's own interpretation of what was learned. It could include gender trends, color preferences, time preferences, driving vs. public transportation, or family dynamics. For example, based on the quantitative example above: *we found that of those who gave new donations, they tended to be single women, above the age of 35 who prefer to donate by credit card instead of by check.*

Strategies & Tactics

Strategies and tactics generally begin with using the research and analysis you received to make judgment calls on how best to achieve the marketing objective. Solid research and analysis will have uncovered who your primary target is, their preferences, and any unique positioning advantages that offer you a dynamic opportunity to come up with a strategy that best communicates what you have to offer to your target.

Your specific tactics could include advertising and various advertising mediums such as radio, television, print or even the Internet. We will explore more strategies and tactics in the "Keys" section of this book where we will take a look at the various individual mediums and their specific benefits to help you make the best strategic decisions on the most effective vehicles for achieving your marketing goals.

Chapter Two:

Making The Shift

"Having the right mindset is a critical part in non-profit marketing. Believe it or not, there is a difference."

This chapter mainly deals with making the transition from corporate marketing to the unique nuances of non-profit and cause marketing. Having the right mindset is a critical part in non-profit marketing. Believe it or not, there is a difference. Although I've worked on the corporate side for more than 20 years, I really do enjoy non-profit marketing. I learned early on that there are some differences and my own mindset had to shift.

What's the difference, you ask? In corporate America it was always about making a profit, increasing market share, brand identity and brand positioning. And yes, those are all important elements in any type of marketing. However, in the non-profit realm, while I may employ these same elements, I receive the added benefit of receiving a much greater joy or measure of success out of making a genuine difference in someone's life.

We definitely want to help the organization raise funds, but we also have this profound opportunity to provoke positive change in our communities through the marketing tactics we utilize to help the organization get the word out about its mission and services.

It's a unique shift as a marketer from solely seeking success to also seeking significance. That's the beauty of what we do as marketers for ministries and non-profit organizations on the marketing side. We have an outstanding opportunity to utilize our gifts, talents, intellect and skills for the greater good. So, our efforts become not so much about making a 'profit' but more about making a 'difference'. That's powerful.

For some, it even equates to a passion. A burning desire, transitioning from something I "can" do to something I "must" do. For some, it's a real challenge making the shift from a corporate marketing mentality to a cause-driven or non-profit marketing mentality, but it can be done.

One thing that has helped me make that shift is a unique phrase from Bishop T.D. Jakes that simply says, "THIS is not THAT". We can't come into this realm trying to make the non-profit fit the corporate mold by which we have become accustomed to. We have to come into this with a degree of respect for the arena and take the time required to learn how things flow in this genre or on this platform. What are the rules of engagement? What are the commonalities? What differences do I see upfront based on my corporate experiences? Then identify those areas where you can help propel the organization forward, one step at a time.

Non-profit or church marketing requires a different thought process because you now have the added element of 'sensitivity' in communicating things the right way to best represent the organization and initiate a response from key donors or supporters. In my opinion, non-profit marketing really stretches your creative abilities because of these sensitivities.

How so? Because this arena does not function with the same types of budgets one would see in the corporate arena. In some cases, there is NO budget. To keep the cause or mission moving forward, we're forced to find creative and productive ways to help get the word out.

Another major difference is the unique audiences we speak to. While a large percentage of traditional marketing is directed towards consumers, in the non-profit world, our "consumers" are most likely donors or clients. Donor response and support is the lifeline to survival for any non-profit organization.

The other key consumer audiences are the clients or members being served. Today, clients and church members have options to choose which organizations they want to attend or interact with. You may not be the only church on your block or the only non-profit organization providing the services you provide. Today, people have a myriad of options and organizations to choose from.

We've all heard the phrase "think outside the box", well; you really have to do this in the non-profit world because there may be times when we can't afford the "box".

As I close this chapter, here are a few key things I've learned about making the shift:

- The organization's staff may not understand traditional, secular business and marketing principles. It's up to you to be the champion who brings education, understanding and enlightenment.

- You have to make time to showcase your results. If you're not telling your own story, someone else will. Keep your donors and staffed informed about your progress. Review your results to help you make better decisions about future efforts.

- Expectations for the marketing team are always high. There may be times when goals may be established on your behalf by a board or committee that may not be feasible in the short term. Set the expectations for any campaign and avoid the trap of having to produce consistent 'miracles'.

- Be upfront about the timelines required to effectively complete the project.

- Be prepared to explain the analysis and strategy considerations required before jumping into projects. Think things through and have a method to the "madness". Remember, we aren't marketing just to do marketing. We're on a mission to get results.

Chapter Three:

First Things First...
Building A Marketing Plan

"An organization that does not plan will consistently find itself like a fireman... always putting out fires."

Often times, in our eagerness to **"do something"** or in our urgency to **"get the word out"**, many organizations fail to take the time needed to actually think through what they're attempting to accomplish. I see so many organizations operate by a fly-by-the-seats-of-your pants type model that ultimately leads to frustration, confusion and burnout for your staff. An organization that does not plan will consistently find itself like a fireman... always putting out fires.

Any organization focused on outreach needs a marketing plan of some type. Today, I want to challenge you to stop, take a deep breath and set aside a few brief moments to strategically think about your organization and its plans.

A good marketing plan sets the direction and focus you need to help accomplish your objective. A good plan will also clarify, (1) where you're going; and (2) give you an indication of when you have arrived at your destination.

Although you should do a comprehensive annual marketing plan for the organization as a whole, I also want to challenge you to consider individual marketing plans for specific events or initiatives that you're planning to undertake.

The elements of a good marketing plan should include the following items:

1. The mission of the organization or the mission of the initiative being undertaken.

2. An assessment of the current business environment, research results and an informed look at the competition.

3. SWOT Analysis (see illustration in this chapter)

4. A flashback of the results from the last time the initiative was undertaken or the organization's overall marketing results/analysis from the previous year.

5. What specific constituent needs should be addressed

6. List of goals. Define what success looks like.

7. What's the strategy or specific steps that will be taken to reach the goals?

8. Prioritize the objectives and benchmarks.

9. Set project due dates and create a timeline.

In a nutshell, a good marketing plan should always help you answer the following questions with some clarity:

- What do we do as an organization? (our focus & mission)
- How do we do it? (resources needed)
- Is it working? (results and challenges)

S.W.O.T ANALYSIS:

If an organization elects not to do a marketing plan, at a bare minimum, I highly recommend at least completing a SWOT analysis. A SWOT analysis is a strategic planning tool to evaluate the Strengths, Weaknesses, Opportunities, and Threats involved in a project or organization. It involves identifying internal and external issues that are favorable or unfavorable to achieve an objective.

1. **STRENGTHS:** characteristics of the business, or project team that give it an advantage over others

2. **WEAKNESSES** (or Limitations): are characteristics that place us at a disadvantage relative to others

3. **OPPORTUNITIES:** external chances to improve organization, performance or revenue opportunities

4. **THREATS:** external elements in the environment that could cause trouble for the organization or project

Empowered Marketing
S.W.O.T. ANALYSIS WORKSHEET

Helpful – to achieving our objectives
STRENGTHS

- _____
- _____
- _____
- _____
- _____

Harmful – to achieving our objectives
WEAKNESSES

- _____
- _____
- _____
- _____
- _____

OPPORTUNITIES

- _____
- _____
- _____
- _____
- _____

THREATS

- _____
- _____
- _____
- _____
- _____

1. **STRENGTHS:** characteristics of the business, or project team that give it an advantage over others
2. **WEAKNESSES** (or Limitations): are characteristics that place us at a disadvantage relative to others
3. **OPPORTUNITIES:** external chances to improve organization, performance or revenue opportunities
4. **THREATS:** external elements in the environment that could cause trouble for the organization or project

Chapter Four:

How Do We Pay For It

"Can you afford NOT to market in this highly competitive economic landscape?"

If there's anything I understand, I completely understand the budget wars from both the church and non-profit management perspective. In this current economy, when organizations are finding their funding reduced or having to face cutting programs and services, marketing/advertising is often the first area recommended for cuts or complete elimination. Yes, marketing and advertising does add to the budget, but the real question is...can you afford NOT to market or advertise in this competitive economic landscape?

It's important to make sure that key decision makers are actively engaged and understand the marketing objectives you want to achieve. Your results, if executed properly, should actually add revenue to the bottom line. In other words, if you look at marketing and advertising as just an expense, you may be missing the big picture.

Marketing and advertising is actually an investment, rather than an expense, that can yield great returns and actually contribute revenue to the organization. I've seen it over and over again, where organizations make significant marketing cuts, only to find that they actually cut off a source of revenue. Marketing is an investment.

Here's what you can achieve with marketing: because there are only so many budget dollars available, it's paramount to engage your audience and your donors in such a way that (1) you standout from the rest;

and (2) makes the donor feel they are supporting an organization that's making a real impact in the area that they're passionate about. This is a winning combination and effective strategy for any execution. People have a plethora of choices and options today on where to spend or donate their dollars. Your task through <u>your</u> marketing is to make sure they choose YOU.

The good news is, you can implement both of these strategies without spending a fortune. I believe in larger-than-life positioning, even with a small budget. Image counts.

Start with the marketing costs and conduct a review of the previous result (if applicable). This historical information will help you in setting an achievable goal for your campaign or marketing program. Next, determine what's needed to recoup the expense (break-even) after factoring in all costs. For example, how many tickets or sponsor ads need to be sold to cover the event costs: If my costs are $2k and my tickets are selling for $20, I need to sell 100 tickets minimum to cover my costs.

Research shows that you consistently average 500 attendees at this event, so in this example, regardless of the expenses, look at the total number of ticket sales needed to cover them, based on your attendance capacity. If in this scenario there are additional budget add-ons, look at how may additional tickets need to be sold to cover those costs.

If you find you have more expenses than you have in total event capacity, it's time to cut the budget. Or if your expenses require more than 50% of your budget, you may need to evaluate if the profit margin is acceptable.

This type of cost-based approach will always help manage expectations and communicate to your management team and decision makers that reaching your objective may be closer and more achievable than they realize. It may be an easier sell to state to them that "our event is projected to earn $10,000 and we are projecting 500 ticket sales. We only need to sell 100 tickets to cover our expenses and anything beyond the first 100 tickets sold is pure revenue. If we hit our projection, we will realize an $8,000 profit."

This kind of communication gets attention and sets expectations up front. Your task as the marketer in this scenario is to make sure you choose an effective strategy that effectively gets you those results and motivates your target audience to get there.

Chapter Five:

Creative Strategies

"Every marketing campaign should have a purpose or goal in mind."

Now that we've taken time to discuss marketing basics and how to fund our efforts, let shift the conversation more to the execution side. When it comes to marketing, you have so many options to choose from in order to effectively engage your audience or constituents. Our discussion about research should have given you some unique insights into discovering and learning more about your audience configuration and their unique habits as well as learning more about your organization. This is the foundation of the choices you will make next in regards to how to best reach your audience.

Every marketing campaign should have a purpose or goal in mind. Although the things we do as churches or non-profits should lead to reaching the lost or assisting those in need, let's try to identify the specific "next steps" you are looking to accomplish through marketing:

- Growth
- Outreach
- Event Attendance
- Name Recognition
- Community Empowerment
- Community Service

Advertising vs. Marketing

This is the age-old question that many marketers face on a consistent basis: advertising vs. marketing. I've seen this question repeatedly as a marketing and advertising professional and it's a valid subject that needs to be communicated. Both components are equally important, but Advertising, in the big picture, can be considered a tool or function of marketing. It's a tactic or a weapon in your arsenal to achieve your objective.

As we've discussed in the previous chapters, Marketing deals more with the systematic planning and determining the who, where and why. Advertising focuses more on the message: It's the part that involves getting the word out concerning your business, product, or the services you are offering. Advertising deals more with "what we say" and "how we say it".

As we move into the next chapter we'll begin to discuss understanding creativity, look at creating a creative brief and dig deeper into the structure of a good advertising or marketing campaign.

Chapter Six:

Understanding Creativity

"One of the best lessons I've learned about advertising is that one ad does NOT fit all."

Everyone reading this book has seen or heard advertising in some form or another. Whether it was the ad you saw while watching your favorite television show, the billboard you passed on the way to work as you were hearing a commercial running on the radio, to the junk mail you may have received in the mail yesterday. All of these are creative executions of someone's marketing plan or strategy.

Careful thought and attention has gone into the design and graphics. A specific reaction or goal from the viewer was thought about and anticipated in advance. The information you gleaned from that ad was strategically selected to run at the right time, in the right place and position to prompt you to take an action. The creative execution of your marketing effort is critical and can be a key factor in the success or failure of the project or initiative.

So, what constitutes a good or bad ad? The opinions may vary widely as creativity is often subjective to individual tastes and preferences. One of the best lessons I've learned about advertising is that one ad does NOT fit all. With this in mind, again, a certain level of forethought and strategy must be considered with every creative project. Every project should begin with a creative brief.

A creative brief sets the creative objectives for the project by expressing the goals, tone, voice and required deliverables or specifications for the ad. Whether you have your own internal graphic artists or if you use external design firms, a creative brief is extremely helpful to the artists in gaining a good understanding of the project as they come up with the best creative concepts to help achieve the goal.

The same creative brief is also helpful to the producer of a television or radio advertisement and gives them the direction they need to effectively execute the project.

Sample Creative Brief Questions:

- What's the situation? What opportunity is being overlooked?
- What are we trying to achieve?
- Who are we talking to?
- What makes them tick?
- What ONE thing are we trying to tell them?
- Why should they believe it? What support, facts, proof, etc., do we have to back up the "one thing"?
- What do we want them to think, feel or do? What is the tone of voice? Are we talking casual, serious, informative, friendly, technical?
- Are there any legal mandates, graphic guidelines or logo requirements?

Creative Brief

Featured Brand? What brand will be featured on this project

Brand Essence: One simple statement or phrase -- that defines the qualities, personality and uniqueness of the brand

What's the situation? Give some background on why we are doing this assignment. What opportunity is being overlooked?

What are we trying to achieve? List the objective or objectives of the assignment.

Who are we talking to? Give the demographics and the psychographics.

What makes them tick? Provide an insight into what motivates our audience. Describe what need or state of need this product/service addresses.

What ONE thing are we trying to tell them? What is the single-most compelling idea we can communicate to get the target from what they currently think to what we want them to think?

Why should they believe it? What support, facts, proof, etc., do we have to back up the "one thing"?

What do we want them to think, feel or do? What is the desired response?

What is the tone of voice? Are we talking casual, serious, informative, friendly, technical?

Are there any legal mandates, graphic guidelines or logo requirements? Think of them now to save frustration later.

Project Budget	
Materials deadline	
Project Start Date	

What Is Creativity?

According to the dictionary: cre·a·tiv·i·ty /krēā'tivitē/

The use of the imagination or original ideas, esp. in the production of an artistic work.

This definition sums it up perfectly. It's the use of the imagination. It's innovation. Just because you're a church or a non-profit organization doesn't mean you can't be creative, modern and relevant in your creative executions. In fact, we should be twice as creative considering that many of our organizations rely on the generosity of others to survive. We have to produce work that is engaging in order to get their attention and communicate our message as we compete against other real world offerings. No more plain, boring ads. I'm encouraging you to step it up!

I'm seeing a trend where some of the larger mega-churches or larger well known non-profit organizations are doing just that…being more creative. From dynamic and colorful brochures to innovative websites, these larger organizations are pulling out all the stops to compete in the marketplace. Bold colors, stimulating graphics, innovative web sites and well-written messages get attention.

But where do you begin? It all starts with the basics we discussed in the form of your marketing plan and a creative brief. Creativity, in summary, involves two processes: Thinking then Producing.

Brainstorming (Thinking)

One of my favorite things to do with my team is to have brainstorming sessions as we develop a creative brief. We all come together in a room with a whiteboard or we use the sticky easel-pads to write all the ideas down. There are no right or wrong answers. In fact, the answers should build off each other to guide you to something that everyone agrees with. One good idea can spur an outbreak of creativity and synergy. Write every idea down and once you're finished brainstorming, recap your final conclusions and brainstorming ideas on a separate, clean document or board. From here, you may have everything you need to complete the creative brief.

Production (Producing)

Once your creative idea is developed, now comes the fun part of getting it produced or created. With a creative brief in hand, any artist or broadcast producer is armed with a powerful tool to bring you success in your effort. Graphic artists should always provide at least 2-3 concepts for you to review and broadcast producers should provide some sort of storyboard or outline of the production.

For radio ads, based on the creative brief, specific talking points may need to be supplied featuring the key messages that need to be communicated. At the heart of all the creative production, make sure you engage a good copywriter who can effectively communicate your message and write in a style that's engaging based on the tone of your message and campaign. As you develop your timelines, make sure you allow adequate time for creative production.

This is why advance planning is critical. An artist who is rushed may not give you his or her best. In addition to graphic production, make sure there's adequate time for any video or audio production as well. Some video projects may require shoots at specific locations as well as time to edit the video in post-production.

Too Much Creativity???

I spent so much time getting you excited about being creative, and now want to discuss the danger of too much creativity. Yes, this can actually happen. New, innovative ideas are the lifeblood of any mission or organization. However, if you're constantly bringing too many new ideas to the table, it could hinder the execution of previous ideas and projects your team is already working on.   I've seen scenarios when organizations focus too much on being creative without any thought about the work required for these new ideas.   They roll out idea, after idea to the point they're stuck with a lot of great new ideas, but limited capacity to implement them all.

This scenario is also common with visionary CEO's and directors who may be out of the overall creative loop and have no idea about your existing projects currently in production.   This is when internal communication becomes critical.   Naturally, we don't want to say "no" to any CEO, but make sure everyone is clear about what's required to implement the new idea and if any existing priorities in production need to be shifted.   If you foresee a potential challenge in executing the new idea, communicate those challenges and let the decision rest with the CEO or manager.

Broken Pieces

In any creative area, there's a potential tendency for your team to get so excited about launching new ideas in lieu of the follow-up and attention needed on existing projects in the works. Be creative, but be strategic with the execution and actively monitor your timetables and workload. A project list or tracker is ideal and a very helpful tool for creative management. Make sure it includes start dates, due dates, assignment by name of the various project tasks and an area for notes & updates.

The cumulative effect of starting too many little projects here and little projects there, of relatively small value, may ultimately lack any profit whatsoever. The same funds and energies that were used for all the little, smaller jobs could have been combined into one unique cohesive strategy that could have been more effective because it was better funded. Planning is essential.

Team Dynamics

As you build your creative team, here you'll find a quick overview of some of the typical key players in the process. While many larger organizations may have actual paid staff performing these functions, I recognize that some smaller organizations may need to utilize freelance help or volunteers. If you are a naturally "task-oriented" person, there is always a temptation to "do it yourself"— and in some scenarios, you may have to! But, pulling together the right team to assist you can help make your projects more successful and less stressful.

If you have to use volunteers to perform these functions, recruit volunteers who are best suited for each of the specified team positions.

Consider the following attributes to look for:
• Specific Gifts
• Special talents
• Availability

- Reliability/commitment
- Willingness to serve
- Ability to lead others or be lead

You never know who may be sitting in your congregation or what gifts and talents may already be waiting for you within your pool of volunteers. You can increase or decrease the size of your team based on the project. In addition, some positions may be combined. For example, you may have access to a graphic artist who is also a good web designer.

Team Dynamics - Key players & functions:

- <u>Graphic Artist:</u> a key team member who comes up with a visual way to represent an idea or concept as a visual representation of your plan and desired result.

- <u>Data & Analysis:</u> this is the person who does the research and provides the data you need to generate a good plan and to measure your success after the execution of a marketing initiative.

- <u>Copywriter:</u> this person writes compelling advertising text (copy) that accurately communicates your message and motivates your audience to take action or experience certain emotions.

- <u>Project Manager:</u> this person organizes people and manages tasks by keeping watch over the project including monitoring start times, due dates and resolving any needs or challenges that may arise in the execution of the project.

- <u>Web/Social Media Team:</u> this team generally includes a Web Designer who is responsible for all of the visual parts of websites while a Web Developer handles more of the technical aspects from e-commerce to writing necessary scripts or building the overall framework for the web site. The Social Media person is responsible for managing and posting all social content and monitoring results.

- <u>Television Production:</u> this team is generally outsourced in many instance but includes the various resources required to complete a production project including a producer, director, film crew and the various technicians required for lighting, sound, graphics, editing and post-production.

Chapter Seven:

Empowered Marketing Keys

"Everybody is talking about social media. If you aren't using social media, you may need to look again."

This chapter is a collection of brief overviews and basic insights into the use of various mediums or me personally sharing some of the things I've learned along the way. Many of these responses have been driven by the questions I've received on an ongoing basis either from my training workshops to one-on-one interactions for insights about marketing and advertising.

You can read them all or refer to the table of contents to jump directly to the particular Empowered Marketing Key that interests you most.

Empowered Marketing Key #1

SOCIAL MEDIA

Everybody is talking about social media. If you aren't using social media, you may need to look again. Online social networks provide exceptional and innovative opportunities for you to interact directly with your audience in a way that's fun and personal.

Through social media, consumers now have a way to engage the companies and brands that are important to them in a meaningful way that's rapidly becoming an integral part of our everyday lives. In fact, the way a person feels about your organization can significantly be impacted via social media as friends share among friends their thoughts, attitudes, opinions and interactions with various companies, brands and services.

According to Nielsen, much of the growth we're seeing in social media has been significantly impacted by the growth in smartphone and tablet usage. Time spent on mobile apps and the mobile web account for 63 percent of the year-over-year growth in overall time spent using social media.

Forty-six percent of social media users say they use their smartphone to access social media; 16 percent say they connect to social media using a tablet. (Nielsen NetView (July 2012), Nielsen Smartphone Analytics (July 2012)

If you don't have a social media strategy in your marketing plans, you may need to reconsider in an effort to remain relevant in these shifting times. In addition to setting up use of social media, it's important to have a strategy to provide content and measure your success.

One strategy I encourage is that you to consider ways you can use the various social media networks synergistically and collectively for a more diversified, cohesive campaign. However, the audience dynamics are different for each network based on individual user preferences.

Just because someone is on Facebook, may not necessarily mean that they're on Twitter or Instagram. In addition, the way you speak to these users or the length of your messaging may be affected by the dynamics and framework of each social network. For example, Twitter has a limit of 140 characters for each post while Facebook allows flexibility to submit longer posts.

These are the top, current social media networks and their user impact:

SOCIAL NETWORK	MONTHLY USERS
FACEBOOK	1.06 billion users
YOUTUBE	1 billion users
TWITTER	500 million users
GOOGLE+	343 million
LINKEDIN	200 million
TUMBLR	170 million
INSTAGRAM	100 million users
BLOGGER	78 million users
WORDPRESS	74 million
PINTEREST	48.7 million
MYSPACE	25 million users
FOURSQUARE	25 million users

The key to good, effective social media is being social. You want to give your followers a sense of relationship and genuine, authentic engagement. It's not just a one-way dialogue, but a rich opportunity to give your organization or brand some personality. These users want to feel that you're communicating directly to them. Another mistake many marketers make is that they over market or use social media strictly for promotion. Today's users want to be engaged, particularly if you can provide content that's of some benefit to them. The goal is to connect with the audience.

The content you provide is critical and should be managed regularly, if not daily. One strategy is the use of a content management software tool like Hoot Suite that allows you to schedule posts across various networks. This type of tool, however, requires some pre-planning and early development of your content.

In summary, develop a social media strategy before you jump in, and avoid the temptation to wing-it or do this haphazardly. I see so many marketers rush to get on social media with no plan or content, then complain that social media does not work. Additionally, have realistic expectations about this medium. Although powerful, and it does offer great promotional and marketing opportunities, at the end of the day, this medium is primarily about communicating info in a "social" fashion.

In addition, a single one-time post on Facebook or Twitter may not yield the type of results that you or others in the organization may expect, compared to more traditional media. It's not uncommon for some to believe that hundreds or thousands will respond to your offer instantly just because you posted it in social media. Factors such as the users own interest, geographic location and personal preferences are all contributing factors to a response. For social media, a good rule of thumb is to remember that you're simply making information available.

Empowered Marketing Key #2

FACEBOOK

Okay, I admit it… of all the available social media tools, Facebook is among my top two favorites. This social network revolutionized the entire social media phenomenon by personalizing the way we communicate with each other in an online environment.

On Facebook, you can share your thoughts; connect with old friends or classmates; post or share your favorite photos or videos; play games or even setup or schedule an event and invite others to participate.

Other users can "like" your posts or your photos and leave comments. This is just a sample of the myriad of functions offered by Facebook.

Not only is Facebook beneficial for individuals, but one of the largest growing user groups on Facebook is companies, organizations and their brands. Facebook offers users a standard user page or you can setup what was once called a "fan" page, which were ideal for companies, brands or public figures.

These "fan" or "like" pages offer an entirely different user experience and present you a unique way to showcase your organization or brand through customization. Customization is extremely important on "fan" or "like" pages as you have the equivalent of a large web banner to promote your organization called a "cover" image. Among the best features for these "like" pages is the ability to run promotions, post events, conduct surveys, run promotional videos, organize photo galleries and target who you communicate with by specific geographic areas.

I remember when I joined the marketing team at TDJ Ministries, there was a Facebook page, but it was initially setup as a standard user page. My first priority was to immediately establish a "fan/like" page to offer us more flexibility to make the ministry more visible. We started with about 3,000 followers initially and within 3-4 years, our followers have grown to more than 1.5 million.

This kind of success was a coordinated team effort. From having a clear strategy of how and when we wanted to communicate to our followers, to having a dedicated focus on developing consistent content featuring inspirational messages from the heart of our leader, we connected with our followers.

My all-time favorite feature on the "like" pages is that Facebook offers you an analytics dashboard.

This dashboard allows me to see what content works based on responses; view how many new followers we are attracting; and see a global geographic view of where our followers are coming from, their gender and what language they speak. It's a powerful tool and a tremendous asset in developing an ongoing growth strategy for Facebook.

A few closing thoughts about Facebook:

- Try to post something at least once daily.
- Content is critical. Invest the time needed to create good content.
- Being social means socializing. Try to engage your followers, not just promote to them.
- If you don't have custom content, use famous quotes, scriptures or memes (images with quotes on them)
- Make sure you post pictures that represent the heart of your organization. People want to learn more about you.

- Facebook allows paid advertising called "Facebook Ads". You can target users who have specific interests and strategically have your ad appear in a designated area on the Facebook interface.

- Visit www.facebook.com to learn more or start your own account.

Empowered Marketing Key #3

TWITTER

Twitter, launched in 2006, is an online social networking service enabling its users to send and receive, short, text-based messages affectionately called "tweets". Twitter has become one of the ten most visited websites on the Internet with over 500 million registered users generating over 340 million tweets daily.

One of the things I really love about Twitter is that it gives my pastor an outlet to connect with a multitude of people that he otherwise may not be able to speak with 1-on-1. Twitter can be a powerful tool for sharing thoughts, inspiration and other information that may be of interest to your audience. Twitter messages tend to be short, sweet and to the point since your posts are limited to only 140-characters.

Every Twitter user has their own, unique Twitter "handle" allowing you to interact with other users by sending a message directly to them using their Twitter handle (Example: @mrtonyscott). All messages are public, but if you and another user are following each other, you can send each other private "direct message".

Although there's a 140-character limit, it's not uncommon to see someone include links inside of their tweet that takes the reader directly to a blog for the full message/article; to a designated website or link them directly to a video you want to share. You can even post a picture with your tweet.

Another powerful tool featured on Twitter is called a "hashtag". Hashtags are displayed with a "#" and a word or short phrase (example: #SundayService). When users search for this particular hashtag, a listing of any tweet using that particular tag will be displayed. This can be a powerful tool to track responses, be it a hashtag used to promote an event or a hashtag referencing your organization.

Progressive churches today are actively using Twitter as part of the worship experience, allowing members to tweet notes or key points the pastor has spoken, utilizing the pastor's Twitter handle and a pre-determined hashtag. If you offer streaming of any type, this is a powerful way to interact with your viewers.

While Twitter has many wonderful aspects, it is a very public platform. Anything you tweet is visible to the world. Pastors and organizational leaders must know the rules of engagement and the public relations risks associated with Twitter. A bad tweet can easily become a public relations nightmare. I've even seen the media on occasion refer to tweets made by public individuals as news to feature in a story. Not to mention some of the public Twitter fights between celebrities that often make headlines.

I caution leaders by telling them to choose their words carefully on Twitter. You can't always respond to drama or every critic since this forum is so public. Recognize Twitter for the world that it resides in. You can see references to God and profanity all in the same posts. Some Twitter handles or hashtags you come across may even give you pause at times. Twitter represents the real power and reality of social media.

To learn more or to start your very own Twitter account, visit www.twitter.com.

Empowered Marketing Key #4

YOUTUBE & VIMEO

Video sharing and viewing on the web has become a normal part of our lives, considering the explosive impact of social media. Video provides an effective and creative way for organizations to communicate to their audience and use video for entertainment, inspiration and as a medium for learning.

In 2011, U.S. adults watched 40.9 billion videos online, an average of 20.5 hours per viewer. Now that video recording equipment is more affordable or even accessible from smart devices, in addition to the ease of use of popular editing software, video is here to stay and likely to increase.

The two primary video hosting websites are YouTube and Vimeo. YouTube is considered the leader in online video considering 1 billion users access this medium every month. Vimeo has more than 60 million unique users every month and caters to a more professional and filmmaking audience based on its clean interface an ease of use.

YOUTUBE INSIGHT

YouTube is a video-sharing website, created in 2005, that allows users to express themselves visually through video. These users can upload, view and share amateur content such as video blogs, short original videos, and educational videos.

While much of the content on YouTube is from individuals, companies and media corporations also offer their material and/or programs on the site. With YouTube, you can create your own channel and post sermons, organizational videos or even fundraising campaign videos. For the best user experience, try to keep your videos short since videos are streamed and your viewers may have variable internet connections and speeds.

Make sure you monitor any comments left about your video for feedback or viewer questions. Also, be aware that after your video has finished playing, other recommended videos will appear and you have no control over what type of videos may be featured. Additionally, because YouTube is free, advertising banners may randomly appear on your video or you may see commercial video clips that run for 15 to 30 seconds before your video starts.

These ads may or may not be related to your organization or its values. The sheer size of the YouTube audience is a plus because of the potential for viewers, but also a negative because the interface can feel a bit cluttered due to all of the user activity and video choices.

VIMEO INSIGHT

Like YouTube, Vimeo is also free, but with a few restrictions and limitations. To expand your capacity on Vimeo, you can purchase paid packages offering more storage space and that speed up your video upload time. Vimeo has a simpler and cleaner aesthetic when you access its pages, making it very easy to search for videos without minimal clutter.

In addition, Vimeo offers a higher video quality with no time limits. Like YouTube, videos from Vimeo can easily be inserted into your social media timelines on Twitter or Facebook.

Empowered Marketing Key #5

INSTAGRAM

Now, we've come to my personal favorite social media application. According to Instagram, it's a "fast, beautiful and fun way to share your photos with friends and family". Because of the various photo filters offered by Instagram, even an amateur or casual photographer can post photos that make them look like a professional photographer.

Instagram allows you to share your photos on several social media networks like Facebook or Twitter. Launched in 2010, Instagram has quickly increased in popularity with over 100 million users each month. In 2012, Instagram was acquired by Facebook.

Like Twitter, Instagram allows the use of hashtags to help users discover certain types of photographs and to communicate directly with each other based on thei personal preferences or social genres they're interested in.

For many, Instagram is a nice change of pace in social networking allowing users to connect and express themselves through photographs, hence the old adage, "a picture says a thousand words". The social power of Instagram gets elevated when users connect in person at "Instameet" events where "Instagramers" come together to socialize while taking photo-walks to capture unique and fun photos.

For organizations or brands, Instagram allows companies to connect directly with their constituents through photography that allows them to show some fun, personality and a human side. Some organizations post "behind-the-scenes" or "exclusive" type of content to drive people directly to Instagram. Instagram can be used to give constituents an exclusive look at events or "day in the life" type of images.

Some great strategies I've seen companies use on Instagram include photo contests, where constituents are encouraged to take photos of a particular brand, utilizing specific hashtags and awarding prizes for the best of the best. For example, Southwest Airlines encouraged their constituents to take and submit their best photos of their experience with the airline, be it a photo of a plane to photos inside the airport that include the Southwest logo. This is just one uniqe example, but the possibilities are endless.

Empowered Marketing Key #6

RADIO ADVERTISING

The Advantages:

Radio can be affordable enough to allow repetition of your message or special offer. You can select a station pretty accurately by its demographics and hone in directly on your target audience. Commercial production costs are low. It's an immediate medium and works very well for promoting events. Radio also complements other advertising and contributes to the multiple message touch-points needed to provoke a response.

The Disadvantages:

Radio impact is limited in that you can't show your product, nor can you expect to communicate a lot of information within a 30 to 60 second window. Audiences of any radio station are geographically scattered and may not be able to take advantage of any location-based offer.

Radio Tips:

- A strong call-to-action is critical to a successful radio ad. This call-to-action should be a phone number or a website to visit.

- Repetition is important. Your radio spot should repeat any key points, particularly, the call-to-action to help listeners recall what they need to do.

- Use of music is very effective in any radio ad. Also the use of humor if appropriate.

- Utilize the station's top DJ personalities to voice-over your spot. Based on the popularity of the DJ, the ad may come across as an endorsement.

- Radio ads should be time-sensitive or date driven. It's important that the listener responds "NOW".

Empowered Marketing Key #7

TELEVISION ADVERTISING

The Advantages:

Television is a medium with high impact. It's possible to purchase airtime in a slot that can be uniquely selected to run at a time when your target audience segment is most likely to be viewing a particular network or show.

The Disadvantages:

TV can be an expensive medium – not only the cost of your airtime, but there may be additional production costs involved to produce and edit an appropriate spot. Cable TV airtime is a little less expensive and offers some unique opportunities based on the multitude of new networks that have come onto the scene and growing in popularity.

Television Tips:

- Television works best when you run multiple ads. One single TV commercial may not yield the results you're looking for.

- National or Network TV buys offers exposure to millions for maximum impact and potential for strong results. However, you may be paying to reach markets that aren't productive for you.

- As an alternative to national or network buys, spot market buys offer an affordable yet effective tool to target specific markets, cities and networks that best reach your constituents.

- The quality of your commercial is essential. It's worth the investment to work with qualified production and post-production companies to help you get a look that's relevant and appealing to viewers.

- TV offers an opportunity to make a strong first impression. Use the opportunity wisely.

Empowered Marketing Key #8

OUTDOOR ADVERTISING

<u>The Advantages:</u>

Offers opportunities to reach a large pool of drivers and/or riders who travel past your billboard every day, which helps to increase your exposure. Billboards can be strategically placed throughout your city base on availability.

<u>The Disadvantages:</u>

Billboard advertising can be expensive and may require a long-term schedule to get the best rates. The average cost of a highway billboard sign, depending on location, may cost anywhere from $1,000 to $5,000 a month depending on size, position and exposure.

Outdoor Advertising Tips:

- Your graphics must be attention getting and stand out in a sea of other billboards.

- Keep your artwork simple. Outdoor ads are only viewed for a few seconds.

- Give just enough information to get attention and push viewers to call or visit your website. You don't have to say everything or your entire message on a billboard, as space and readability are very limited.

- Consider buying these new Electronic Billboards. Your ad can be strategically moved to various electronic boards throughout the city and these boards may cost less than traditional boards.

- As a non-profit, don't be afraid to ask for bonus boards or non-profit discounts.

Empowered Marketing Key #9
PRINT ADVERTISING

In these advancing digital times, there are some who feel that print advertising is on a rapid decline and going out of style. Research shows there are still 187 million magazine reading adults in the U.S. and 46% of them are interacting with their favorite magazines exclusively in print, according to a survey. When asked why they are not currently reading magazine content digitally, the majority (54%) say they "just prefer reading printed copies of magazines," and 44% claim "no interest in reading their magazines in a digital format." (Affinity American Magazine Study, Fall 2011)

There is still an audience for print advertising and a unique opportunity to strategically integrate a digital strategy along with your print strategy to continue the engagement online through QR codes offering exclusive, additional content found only on the web in the form of videos or downloads. A QR Code (Quick Response Code) is a barcode that can be scanned by QR scanner applications on smartphones or tablets. The code can take the user directly to a website, a pdf document or directly to a video.

The Advantages:

Print media (newspapers and magazines) generally has a loyal readership, allowing advertiser to target specific affinity groups (women, business, athletics, etc.) or reach specific geographical areas. Based on budget, you can choose the size of your ad or where you position your ad. Print publications tend to have a longer life because they physically remain accessible, even months after your ad has run.

The Disadvantages:

Can be expensive for national magazines or newspaper ads. Publishers produce editorial calendars in advance, requiring advertisers to plan ad placements several months in advance. Offers little flexibility for tight deadlines. Potential for ads to get lost in the clutter of feature stories and ads from other advertisers. Your ad design can have a potential negative impact on the response to your ad.

Print Advertising Tips:

- Your ad must be designed to get attention and to get a response. Always include a call-to-action be it a phone number or web address.

- Large, bold headlines and a visually appealing image will get readers attention. Keep your artwork and text simple and avoid temptation to over-communicate. Give just enough to peak interest and let them get the rest online or by phone. Use QR Codes to expedite response.

- Plan in advance and create a schedule showing all your ad buys, materials due dates and publish dates. Because of ad costs, research the publication's reach and audience data.

- Discounts offered for multiple insertions. Inquire about non-profit discounts or free ads.

Empowered Marketing Key #10
EMAIL MARKETING

By now, everyone knows what email is and many of you don't like receiving spam. While some suggest that email is going out of style, a 2012 survey of consumer channel habits and preferences found 77% preferred to receive permission-based promotions via email; only 6% preferred such messages via social media. The Direct Marketing Association (DMA) puts email marketing's ROI for 2011 at $40.56 for every $1 invested.

Statistics like these help keep email on the forefront as a viable marketing tool to communicate with new and existing constituents. In addition, the surging and explosive popularity of social media is actively contributing to the ongoing use of email. For your email campaigns to be effective, your eblasts should be appealing and brief. Well written emails often get better responses. Personalization is also a powerful tactic to employ in the use of emails. Your constituents are more likely to respond when they feel you're talking directly to them.

If you don't have a strong infrastructure or database for email, I highly recommend the use of an email service provider like Constant Contact or Get Response. These applications are affordable based on the size of your database and offer many customization options and help you remain compliant concerning the rules and requirements for opt-in and opt-out standards.

These programs also offer you the ability to add graphics to your emails, design e-newsletters and to target specific geographic areas or sub-groups you may have setup in your database.

Empowered Marketing Key #11
WEB SITES

Ironically, as I was writing this particular section, a friend who owns a business called me to get my opinion about building a quick website for his business. He had been wanting a site for some time and now, his business has reached a point to where it is vitally necessary.

The process took so long because he could not decide exactly what he wanted to do. First he wanted a blog. Then, he wanted a full web site, but later realized he had no content. Next, he wanted just a single "coming soon" landing page to serve as a placeholder on his site until the actual site could be built. I watched this battle play out over several weeks until I finally received a phone call.

He had agreed to just initially do a blog type site. So, I recommended Wordpress, a free resource to build your own personal blog (www.wordpress.com). Wordpress would give him the simplicity of a blog, but the look of an actual web site based on the free templates they offer with various themes.

The plan was moving along very well until one of his customers offered to help. This customer had a relative who supposedly knew how to build web sites. My friend got so excited about this opportunity and was about to surrender all of his web credentials. But thankfully, he called me first. I told him to stop the presses and asked him, "have you even seen any of this man's work?" His answer was "no, but he builds websites...".

I was astounded. Don't trust your website development to just anyone. Just like you are selective about any doctor or dentist who treats you, you should be just as selective about who you select to create content for your business. At least view their portfolio or check some references first.

I can't tell you how many times I've seen this situation. In business today, your web site is one of the first and most viewed representations of your organization. The general public will most likely see your website first. If you think a new visitor to your church or agency is connecting with you for the first time, you may be mistaken. Chances are, they probably already visited you first on the web. In other words, in many cases, your web site is a FIRST impression of your organization.

Because your website is a visual representation of your organization, as a result, this representation becomes a direct reflection of you as an organization. My question to you today is when someone looks at your website, what do they see? Is your site appealing and inviting? Or, is it busy and chaotic?

I've seen some interesting web sites over the years. From typos, unattractive designs, links that don't work and my pet peeve above all…a lack of any contact information… Yes, I've seen it all.

A good web site should be:

- Visually appealing
- Easy to navigate
- Functional
- Informative
- Keeps visitors interested
- Constantly updated with information to give visitors a reason to return regularly

Every web site should have at a minimum:

- Info about your organization
- Your contact information
- Ability to capture the visitor's information or a means for them to ask you questions
- An overview of the services you offer

Website Design Tips:

1. View your site from the perspective as if you've never seen it before. Pretend you're the customer:

    a. Navigate your site and see if everything is easy to find.

    b. Avoid too much clutter.

    c. Don't just think about what you like or your own personal preferences. Have your constituents in mind and make sure your site meets their needs for visiting you online.

    d. Make sure your design represents your brand very well.

2. Be creative, but don't go overboard with the design.

    a. Don't overdo your site with too many pictures and very little text.

    b. Color is good, but be somewhat conservative using a few key colors in your design. Too much color could be a deterrent.

3. Content is king.

    a. Make sure your content is updated regularly, relevant and applicable to your constituency.

    b. If you're promoting events, make sure you remove the information after the event has occurred.

4. Make sure your site can be found. Work with your developer on search engine optimization (SEO) and other unique ways to make sure you're visible.

Empowered Marketing Key #12

10 MONEY-SAVING IDEAS & STRATEGIES

1. When you print, try to print in larger quantities to get the best rates. Ask your printer if they offer a weekly "gang run" where multiple print jobs are all run at the same time on a large press.

2. For additional printer savings, consider designing your projects at dimensions that allow 2-up or 3-up printing, which allows you to print more for less. Use of alternative paper stocks can also offer savings. Ask your printer about options available to you.

3. To save money on television ads, consider late night TV buys or excess inventory buys as an option. Purchasing spot market buys in your top markets versus national ads offers significant savings and better opportunities to hit your strongest audience concentrations.

4. To save on direct mail advertising, consider launching your campaign by specific zip codes or targeted regions within a zip code or designated neighborhoods within a zip code to save resources.

5. Electronic billboards may offer more impressions and savings compared to stationary boards.

6. Need affordable graphics help? Consider using freelance artists from art schools or fine arts college students who need work hours or internships to complete their studies.

7. When buying magazine or newspaper ads, plan ahead and group your buys to take advantage of savings offered for multiple insertions.

8. Don't be afraid to ask for a nonprofit rate. Many vendors may offer a discount.

9. If you're tax exempt, keep your exemption documents handy to save on sales tax. Equip your key staff with copies for purchases at office supply stores or quick print shops like FedEx Office to save on taxes.

10. Looking for a quick, affordable way to launch a website? Consider using pre-formatted website templates to save. Many internet service providers (ISP's) and web hosting companies offer web-builder type software with easy to program templates that may meet your immediate needs.

Chapter Eight:

Conclusion

This chapter concludes our Empowered Marketing journey. I hope this book has proven valuable to you and at least provided a few helpful tips or strategies that you can immediately implement to assist your organization.

These are challenging times for many churches and non-profits. But, at the same time, this is also a dynamic time, filled with an abundance of opportunities and possibilities for those organizations that take the lead, focus strategically and uncover new, innovative ways to move ahead of the pack and remain on the forefront of relevance.

Don't neglect any of these advances in technology and social media that offer great opportunities to advance your organization. Embrace them with all diligence to position your organization on the cutting-edge and at the forefront of creativity in constituent engagement.

May God bless your works and abundantly supply everything you need to achieve your organization's immediate goals and mission. We're all in this together, so feel free to share these resources or gift this book to fellow co-laborers in the church or non-profit field who could benefit from this information.

It's been my pleasure to serve you through this book. For occasional tips and marketing insights, please be sure to visit my website at www.empoweredmarketing.org or follow me on Twitter: @mrtonyscott.

About The Author:

Anthony Scott (Tony) is Director of Marketing & Creative Strategy for T.D. Jakes Ministries. In this capacity, he oversees and develops strategies for national ministry outreaches, donor development and television.

With more than 20 years of experience in advertising and marketing, Tony has developed strategic solutions to build and market international brands among consumers. He has been recognized nationally for his keen insights and accurate knowledge of consumer behavior and speaks frequently to companies and organizations about marketing.

An entrepreneur and former ad agency owner, Tony has been featured in Adweek Magazine, The Dallas Business Journal and the Ad Business Report. An active member of his community, Tony has served on several non-profit boards including President/Chair of The Dallas Advertising League, a local chapter of the 50,000 member American Advertising Federation.

www.empoweredmarketing.org

www.ingramcontent.com/pod-product-compliance
Lightning Source LLC
Chambersburg PA
CBHW060624210326
41520CB00010B/1469